Southern Gospel Music And Proud of It

A Collection of America's Best

T0053148

A *J. Aaron Brown & Associates* Publication
in association with

HAL•LEONARD® CORPORATION

960 EAST MARK STREET P.O. BOX 227 WINONA, MN 55987

CONTENTS

HE'S STILL WORKIN' ON ME

Words and Music by
JOEL HEMPHILL

1. There real-ly ought to be a sign up-on my heart, "Don't judge him yet, there's an un-fin-ished part." But I'll be per-fect just ac-cord-ing to His plan, fash-ioned by the Mas-ter's lov-ing hand. He's still work-in' on me to make me what I ought to be. It took Him just a week to make the moon and stars, the

5

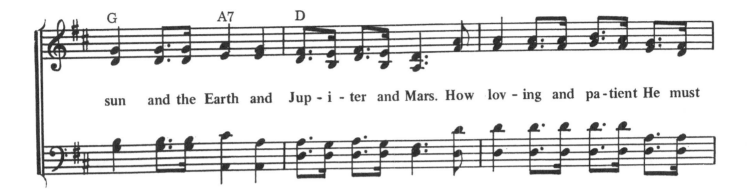

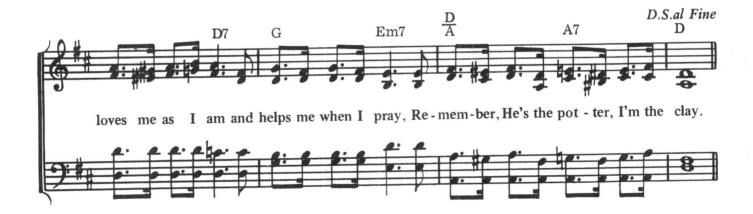

WHEN HE WAS ON THE CROSS

(I WAS ON HIS MIND)

Words and Music by RONNIE HINSON
and MIKE PAYNE

1. — I'm not on an e- go trip; I'm noth- ing on my own,
2. The look of love was on His face, — thorns were on His head,

Make mis- takes, I of- ten slip, just com- mon flesh and bones;
Blood was on His scar- let robe, — stained a crim- son red;

But I'll prove some- day just why I say I'm of a spe- cial kind,
— — Though His eyes were on the crowd, He looked a- head in time,

For when He was on the cross, I was on His mind.
And when He was on the cross, I was on His mind.

OLD-FASHIONED WAY

Words and Music by
JEFF GIBSON

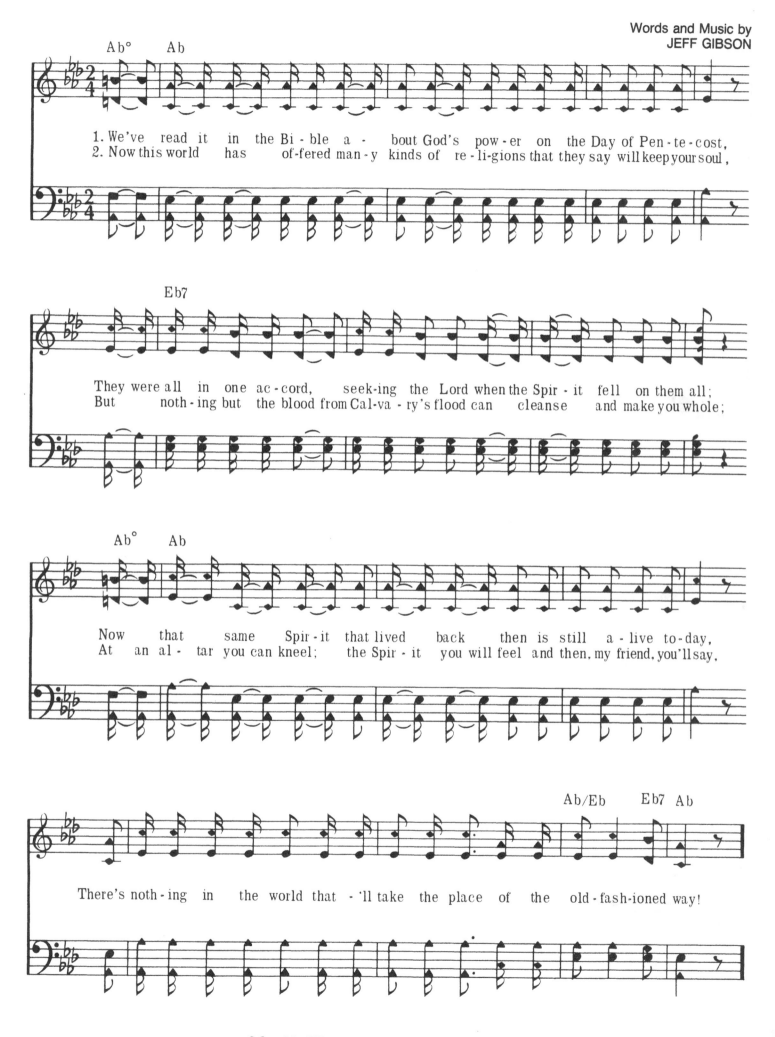

1. We've read it in the Bi-ble a-bout God's pow-er on the Day of Pen-te-cost,
2. Now this world has of-fered man-y kinds of re-li-gions that they say will keep your soul,

They were all in one ac-cord, seek-ing the Lord when the Spir-it fell on them all;
But noth-ing but the blood from Cal-va-ry's flood can cleanse and make you whole;

Now that same Spir-it that lived back then is still a-live to-day,
At an al-tar you can kneel; the Spir-it you will feel and then, my friend, you'll say,

There's noth-ing in the world that -'ll take the place of the old-fash-ioned way!

CHORUS

HE MADE A WAY

Words and Music by
SQUIRE PARSONS

1. There've been times that I've been backed___ up to the wall,
2. Now I know there'll be times when the road will get rough___

There've been times it seemed___ I would___ sure-ly___ fall;
And___ all of us feel like, at times___ giv-ing up;___

When it seemed___ that there___ was no es-cape at___ all,___
But re-mem-ber, my friend,___ He knows when we've had e-nough,___

He made a way for___ me.___
He'll make a way for___ me.___ He made a

CHORUS

GOOD OLD BOYS

By EDDIE CARSWELL

CHORUS

Good old boys won't make it in-to heav-en, good old boys won't wear a crown, Good old boys won't live for-ev-er where the saints of God are found; So don't you dare be mis-led; on-ly Je-sus gives real joy,

'Cause you can take it from me, 'cause I used to be a good old boy! boy!

STANZAS

1. -- Good old boys, they come a dime a doz - en,
2. The week - end comes and they're out on the road a - gain,

do - in' good, good as they care to be;
Way - lon and Wil - lie play - in' on the rad - i - o;

And ev - 'ry - bod - y loves to be a - round them, 'Cause a good old boy, he'd
They worked all week, and they did-n't cheat one per - son, 'Cause a good old boy, he's

never harm a flea;
But the on - ly Lord they know is their
good, don't you know!
But Sun - day's just a day like an - y
CODA Good old boys, I beg you to heed my

plea - sure,
'Cause they live their lives of things that they en - joy,
oth - er,
It's a day for fun and the things they en - joy,
warn - ing,
'Cause ver - y soon we're gon - na see the Lord,

And when you ask a - bout their love for Je - sus,
And when you ask just why they nev - er come a - round,
And when He asks us why you should go to heav - en,

they say, "Don't wor-ry 'bout me, I'm just a good old boy! Good old boys
they say, "Don't wor-ry 'bout me, I'm just a good old boy! Good old boys
-- well, I pray you won't say, "I've been a good old boy!" Good old boys

YOU CAN WALK ON THE WATER

Words & Music by
JON MOHR and JOHN ROSASCO

EMPTY VESSEL

Words and Music by
FELECIA SHIFLETT

1. As my feet walk thru dry and bar-ren plac-es
2. As the mul-ti-tude that day came to-geth-er,

And my soul has felt no rain for a while;
By the sea of Gal-i-lee they all did feast;

But I be-lieve in the wid-ow's emp-ty bar-rels,
But I be-lieve I'm like those lit-tle loaves and fish were,

- She had faith e-nough to bring a vast sup-ply.
And just your touch can mul-ti-ply the ver-y least.

GONNA BE MOVING

By RANDELL HYLTON

1. This ole world's no place for liv-ing, not e-nough care and not e-nough giv-ing,
2. There won't be no time for cry-ing, no more sick-ness, toil, or dy-ing,

Some-times clouds of sin and sor-row hide the way;
Joy a-waits me in the man-sion far a-way;

But this life of storm-y weath-er ain't a-gon-na be my home for-ev-er,
When I rest from all my la-bor, — the Lord will be my next-door neigh-bor,

Gon-na be mov-in', one of these days.
Gon-na be mov-in',

CHORUS

Gon - na be mov - in', mov - in' a - way,
I'm a gon - na be mov - in', mov - in' a - way,

Gon - na be mov - in' one of these days!
Gon - na be mov - in' one of these days!

When I leave this life be - hind me, trou - ble and care are nev - er gon - na find me,

Gon - na be mov - in', one of these days.
Gon - na be mov - in',

HE SPEAKS TO ME

Words and Music by
TANYA GOODMAN

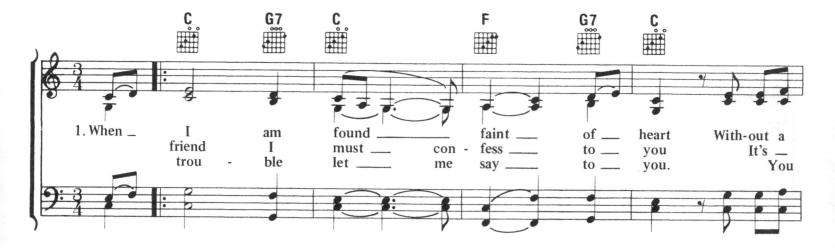

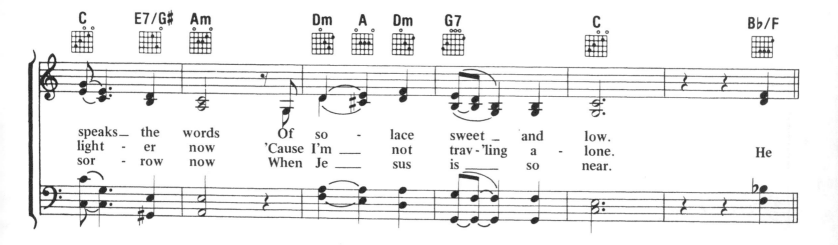

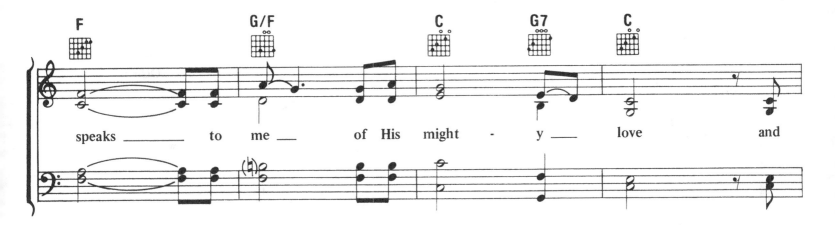

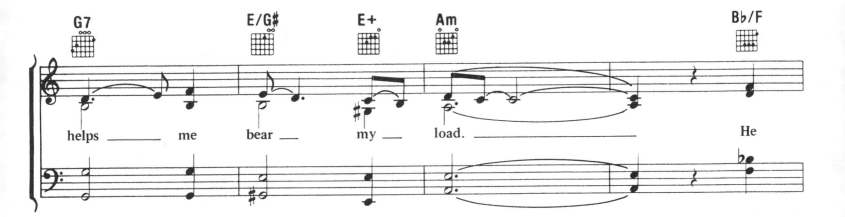

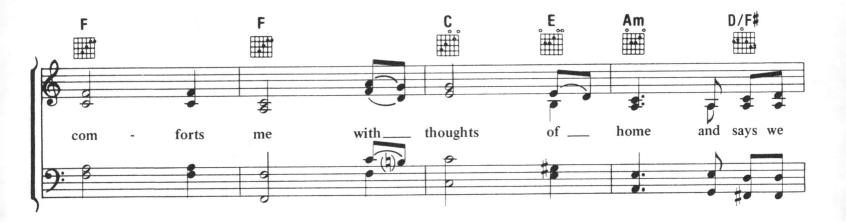

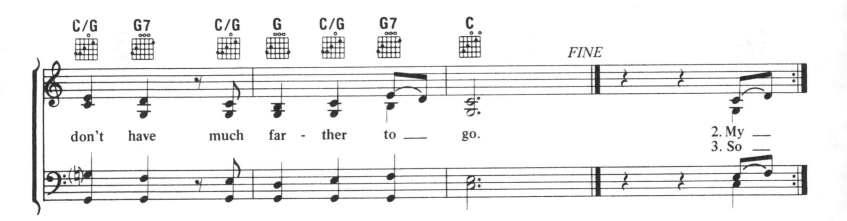

JOHN SAW

Words and Music by
SQUIRE PARSONS

NEW GRACE

Words and Music by
TOM HAYES

1.. All of grace___ is my sto-ry, all the way from earth to glo-ry,
2. There's been grace for ev-'ry tri-al, there's been grace for ev-'ry mile,___

Since by grace He lift-ed me from sin and woe.___
There's been grace suf-fi-cient from His vast sup-ply;___

Liv-ing grace He has ex-tend-ed as on Him my heart de-pend-ed,
Grace to make my heart more ten-der, grace to love and pray for sin-ners,

And He'll give new grace when it's my time to go.___
But there'll be new grace when it's my time to die.___

CHORUS

Grace not yet dis-cov-ered, grace not yet un-cov-ered,

Grace from His boun-ti-ful store;____

Grace to cross the riv-er, grace to face for-ev-er,

There'll be new grace I've not need-ed be-fore.____

THANK GOD I MADE IT

Words and Music by
GENE ANDERSON

1. As my soul left my bod-y that was made of earth-ly clay, An an-gel of the Lord car-ried me through the east-ern gate. As His nail-scarred hands ca-ressed my soul, - He gave me a clean, white robe and I cried, "I've made it! Thank God, I've made it! My feet have touched the streets of gold."

2. Now, my earth-ly life is o-ver, I have made the nar-row way And a crown of life I'm wear-ing down the streets of gold to-day. I'm now tour-ing that ho-ly cit-y, shout-ing down an end-less road

CHORUS

Streets of gold I now am walk - ing, just passed by the tree of life;

Took a drink of liv-ing wa-ter flow-ing down from God on high.

I now see the hal-le-lu - jah square and the man-sion that

won't grow old And I cried, "I've made it! Thank God, I've

made it! My feet have touched the streets of gold."

O FOR A THOUSAND TONGUES

By DAVID BINION

PUT SOMETHING BACK

By JOE HUFFMAN
and CHARLES AARON WILBURN

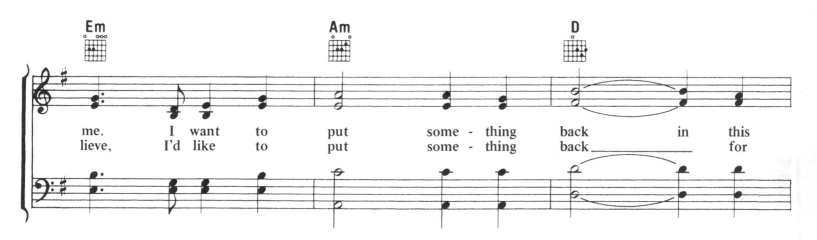

me. I want to put some - thing back in this
lieve, I'd like to put some - thing back ___ for

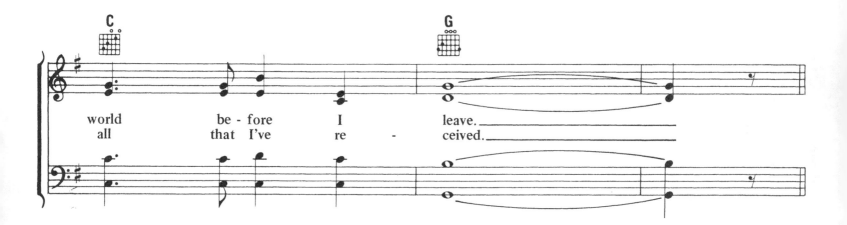

world be - fore I leave. ___
all that I've re - ceived. ___

CHORUS

I want to put some - thing back in this

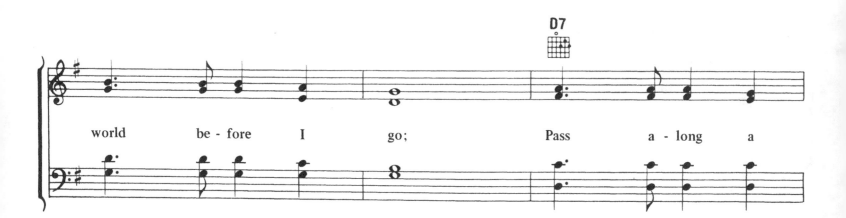

world be - fore I go; Pass a - long a

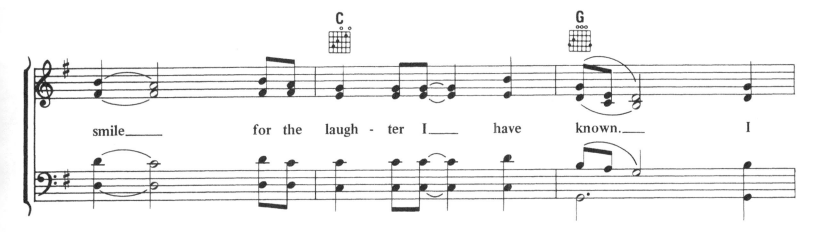

smile_____ for the laugh-ter I____ have known.____ I

love the life I'm liv - ing,_____ I need to show it by____ my

giv-ing; I want to put some-thing back be-fore__ I

go._____ 2. I have go._____

A DIFFERENT WAY

Words and Music by
JEFF GIBSON

1. Now, the wise men went a seek-ing for the Sav-ior had been born
2. From, a babe born in the man-ger to the Man of Gal-i-lee

— And they knew that old king Her-od was out to take a-way our Lord;
He healed the sick and saved the sin-ners, and set the cap-tive free;

When they found the ba-by Je-sus, knelt be-side Him in the hay,
So, no mat-ter where you're head-ed, come to Je-sus to-day

Then they left . . . . a dif-f'rent way.
And you'll leave . . . . a dif-f'rent way.

LET YOUR LIVING WATER FLOW

By JOHN WATSON

CHORUS

Je - sus, Je - sus, _____ Je -

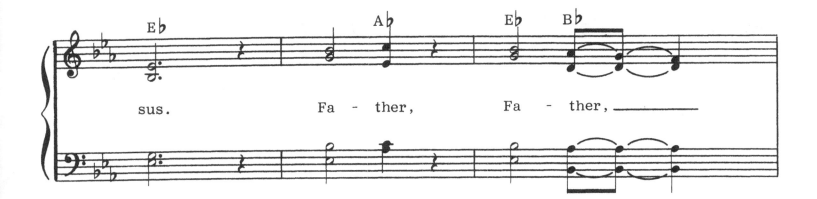

sus. Fa - ther, Fa - ther, _____

Fa - ther. Spir - it,

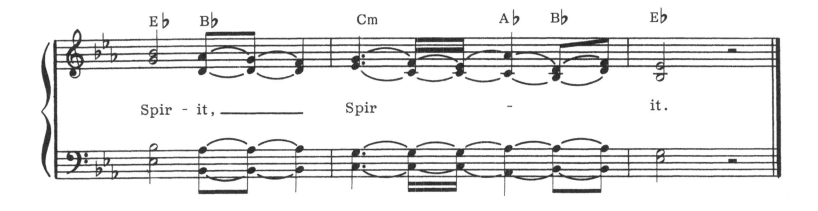

Spir - it, _____ Spir - it.

WHO PUT THE TEARS

By CAROL BASS

Who put the tears _____ in the eyes of the Lamb? _____ Who crowned the head with thorns 'til it bled of the great _ I Am? Who drove the nails _____ in His lov - ing hands; _____ down through the years, who put the tears in the eyes of the Lamb? _____ As Je-sus was walk-ing the last mile to Cal-va-ry's

hill, _____ Pet-er had de-nied Him, they cried, "Cru-ci - fy Him," but

He was in His Fa-ther's will. As He hung in si - lence, our

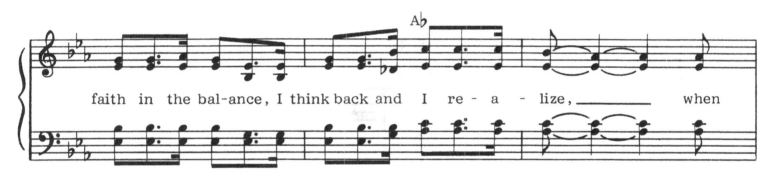

faith in the bal-ance, I think back and I re - a - lize, _____ when

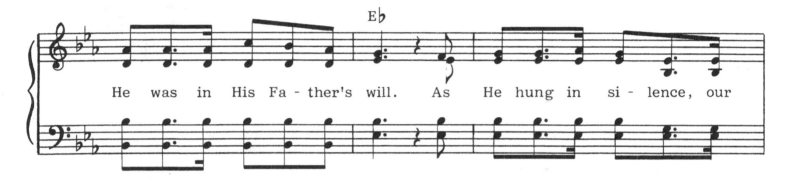

He said, "For-give them," and cried, "It is fin-ished," there were tears in my Fa-ther's

eyes. |2. Eb   D.S. ||3. Eb
Lamb? _____   Lamb? _____

WHEN I RECEIVE MY ROBE AND CROWN

By GEORGE SHUFFLER

AN OLD CONVENTION SONG

Words and Music by
TIM LOVELACE & ROGER JERRY POWELL

1. We used to come from miles a - round, have dinner on the ground under
2. Gos - pel songs to - day have a lot to say, they lift you

neath those old shade trees And sing the old songs in shaped notes, in
up when you're feel - ing down. Some have a coun - try fla - vor,

four part har - mo - ny; Like "He Set Me Free," and "He'll Pi - lot Me," and
some have a mod - ern sound. They all serve a need of plant - ing seeds, so I

"An - y - where Is Home." How long has it been since you heard an
know they can't go wrong But there's none so dear as when I hear an

JERICHO

By ANN BALLARD
and BILL BOOHER

Jer- i- cho!   Jer- i- cho!

1. God said to His peo- ple,   "Pos- sess the prom-ised land;   Move on   in, take
2. We, His cho- sen peo- ple,   — need to move a- head;   Thru the   walls of

Jer- i- cho; I've placed her in   your hands";   She was   a might- y cit- y
fear and doubt to vic- to- ry   be led;   — We must keep on   march-ing

sur- round- ed   by a wall,   But   God said, "Sev- en   times a-round   and
— till the   wall comes down,   — God said to go for- ward;   He

she will sure- ly fall!"
did- n't say turn a- round! Jer- i- cho, Jer- i- cho, cit- y of re- nown,

Josh- u- a led the Is- rael- ites sev- en times a- round;

Jer- i cho, Jer- i- cho, sev- en times a- round, They marched and

then the might- y walls Did come tum- bl- ing down! down!

HOLY GROUND

By GERON DAVIS

1. As I walked thru the door, I sensed His presence,
2. In His presence there is joy — beyond measure,

— And I knew this was a place where love abounds;
And at His feet peace of mind can still be found;

For this is the temple; Jehovah God abides here,
If you have a need, I know He has the answer,

And we are standing in His presence on holy ground!
Reach out and claim it; you are standing on holy ground!

CHORUS

We are stand- ing on ho- ly ground,

And I know that there are an- gels all a- round;

Let us praise Je- sus now,

We are stand- ing in His pres- ence on ho- ly ground!

God Bless The U. S. A.

Words and Music
LEE GREENWOOD

CHORUS
And I'm proud to be an A- mer- i- can where at least I know I'm free, And I

won't for- get the men who died who gave that right to me; And I'd glad- ly stand up

next to you and de- fend her still to- day, 'Cause there ain't no doubt I love this land ——

God bless the U. S. A.! 2. From the U. S. A.!

FEELS ALRIGHT

By RANDY BUXTON

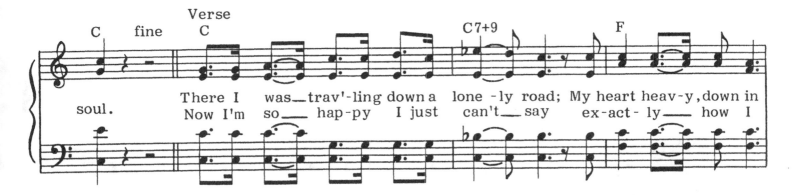

There I was traveling down a lonely road; My heart heavy, down in
Now I'm so happy I just can't say exactly how I

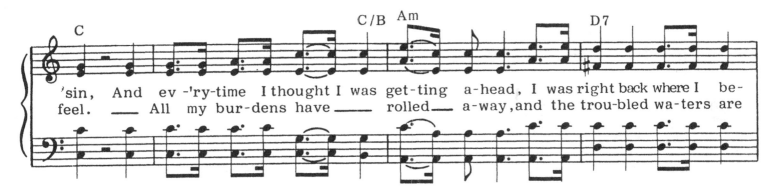

'sin, And ev'ry-time I thought I was getting ahead, I was right back where I began;
feel. All my burdens have rolled away, and the troubled waters are

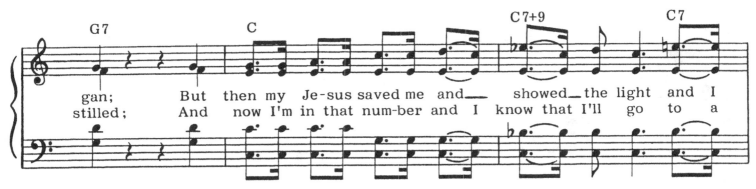

gan; But then my Jesus saved me and showed the light and I
stilled; And now I'm in that number and I know that I'll go to a

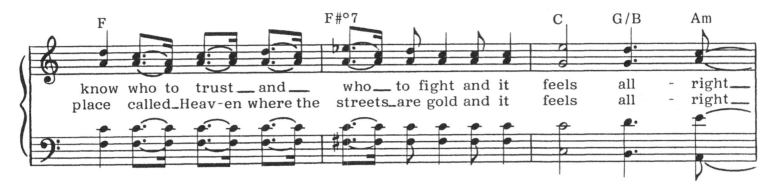

know who to trust and who to fight and it feels all-right
place called Heaven where the streets are gold and it feels all-right

since Jesus saved my soul.

CANAANLAND IS JUST IN SIGHT

Words and Music by
JEFF GIBSON

1. Mos - es led God's chil - dren, for - ty years he led them through the
2. 'Tho we walk thru val - leys, 'tho we climb high moun - tains, we must

cold and through the night. ___ 'Tho they said, "Let's turn back," Mos - es said, "Keep go - ing,
not give up the fight. ___ We must be like Mos - es, we must keep on go - ing,

Ca - naan - land is just in sight."
Ca - naan - land is just in sight. ___ There will be no sor - row there in that to - mor - row,

we will be there by and by. ___ Milk and hon - ey flow - ing,

there is where I'm go - ing, Ca - naan - land is just in sight. ___

I'M IN THIS CHURCH

Words and Music by
JOEL HEMPHILL

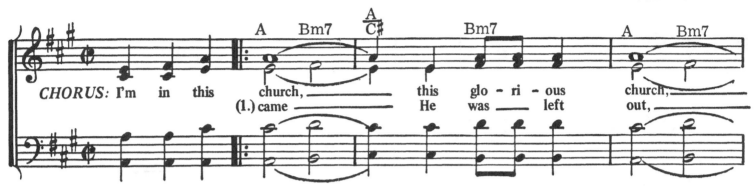

CHORUS: I'm in this church, _____ this glo - ri - ous church, _____
(1.) came _____ He was _____ left out,

_____ I did - n't join, oh, I was born _____ I've had a new birth. _____
_____ there was no place where He was wel - come here on _____ earth. _____

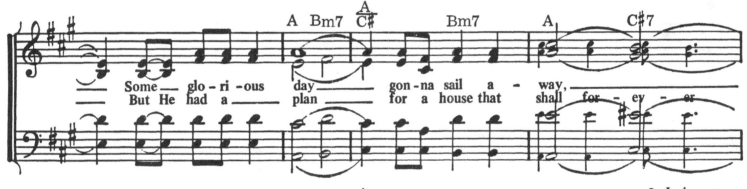

Some - glo - ri - ous day _____ gon - na sail a - way, _____
But He had a _____ plan _____ for a house that shall for - ev - er

_____ it's by His grace, _____ not by my word _____ I'm _____ in this
stand, He spoke these words, _____ "Up - on this rock _____ I'll build my

church. _____ 1. When _____ Je - sus
church. " _____ CHOR. And I'm in this

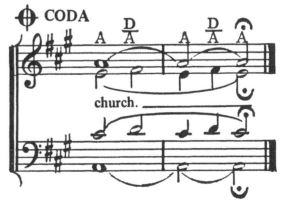

church. _____

WE ARE THOSE CHILDREN

Words and Music by
JEFF GIBSON

1. They fled from E-gypt with old Pha-roah be-hind,
2. You may be walk-ing where it's dust-y and dry,

-- Hop-ing the prom-ised land soon they would find;
But soon we shall gath-er by the Riv-er of Life;

-- God's cho-sen peo-ple, they were will-ing to stand,
With saints of all a-ges we'll be sing-ing a-loud,

They would not give up till they reached that fair land.
We are those chil-dren God brought out.

CHORUS

We are those chil - dren the Bi - ble talks a - bout,

Just like those chil - dren Mo - ses led out;

Well, we've been in the wil - der - ness for much too long,

But we are God's chil - dren; soon we'll be home.

JESUS IS THE LIGHT

By DANNY W. MYRICK

1. — Rid- ing down a lone- ly high- way, not know- ing where to
2. Your friends have all for- sak- en you, and you don't know where to

go, I was search- ing for some an- swers to what ques- tions
turn, You keep try- ing world- ly plea- sures, and it seems you'll

I did- n't know; The world was clos- ing in,
nev- er learn; That the road of sin is rough and long

and there was no hope in sight, — When I heard a voice
like you're driv- ing on a rain- y night, But there's on- ly one — — true

call- ing me, say- ing, Je - sus is the Light!
way, my friend, you see,

CHORUS

Je-sus is the Light, in a world so full of dark - ness, He's the on - ly One you can turn to when you've got no place to go; If you're walk - ing a - long in dark - ness be - cause sin is blind- ing your sight, Don't try to go it on your own, be - cause Je - sus is the Light!

Light! Je - sus is the Light!

WE SHALL BEHOLD THE KING

By DAVID and BOBBY BINION, JR.

CHORUS

STEP INTO THE WATER

By KIRK TALLEY

IT'S ALMOST OVER
(We Are Going Home)

Words and Music by
ANN BALLARD

1. The winds of war keep rag - ing through _____ the
2. We're liv - ing with the great - est prom - ise -

land, _____ far and near; The cry of hun - gry
we _____ will ev - er know, The prom - ise came from

chil - dren, _____ the pain, the fall - ing tears.
heav - en _____ of bless - ed peace and hope.

Na - tions gath - er 'round _____ the ta - ble, for
Bat - tles may keep rag - ing high - er but

peace _____ they've tried for years, Yet war still ra - ges
we _____ will nev - er fear. The Sa - vior's arms are

WAKE UP CHURCH

Words and Music by
SYLVIA GREEN

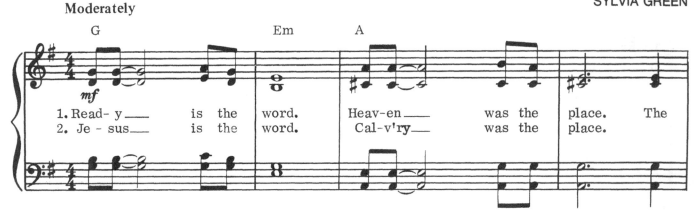

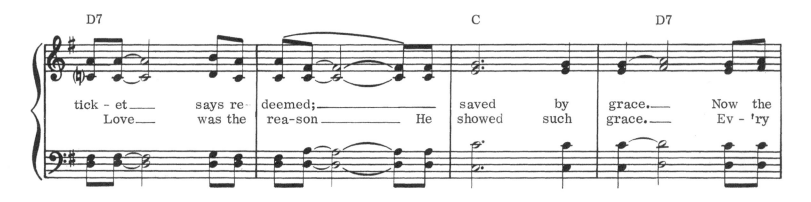

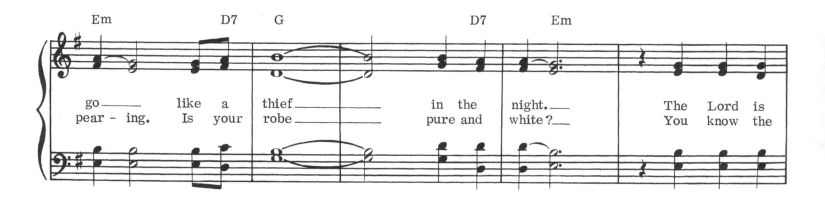

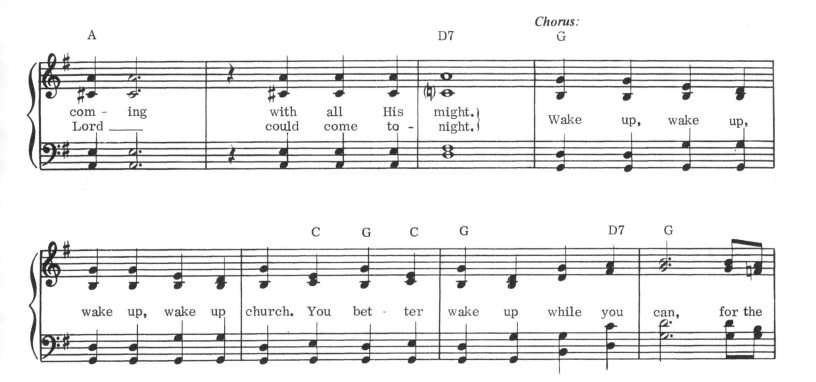

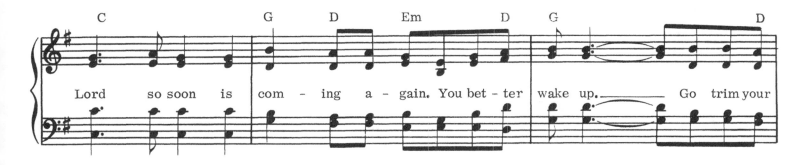

PLACE WHERE THE HUNGRY ARE FED

By AILEENE HANKS

1. Five loaves and two fish - es were brought by a child. He
2. My spir - it is hun - gry, my bod - y grows weak; I've
3. There's no need for can - dles, the Lamb is the light; No

broke it and blessed__ it and__ ten - der - ly smiled;__ And
fol - lowed the mul - ti - tudes, for the Mas - ter I see.__ There's
sun - set, no sun - rise, for__ nev - er comes night.__ All

there on the sea - shore, the sup - per was spread at the
no need to hur - ry, it's just up a - head, it's the
things are now read - y, the Lamb shall be wed in this

place where the hun - gry were fed._____
place where the hun - gry are fed._____ There were
place where the hun - gry are fed._____

CHORUS

mil - lions be - fore me. but there's no wait - ing line. __ There's a

place at His ta - ble, and I know that it's mine. No

crumbs from His ta - ble, Still I must be led to the

place where the hun - gry are fed. _____

HELLO MAMA

Words and Music by
SQUIRE PARSONS, JR.

MY HEART IS ALREADY HOME

By KYLA ROWLAND

1. More and more I feel like a stran-ger there's so much I don't un-der-
2. I can't seem to get ac-quaint-ed with this style of liv-ing to-

stand! Why a world so lost would not want a Sav-ior, and
day; For my mind just keeps on wan-d'ring up to

not want to take His hand; It's not for me to
where my trea-sures are laid; I can al-most see to the

ques-tion, so I leave it with One who knows, Oh, my heart is no
beau-ty, and at times I can hear the songs, I can stay in

long- er of this world; — it left here a long time a- go!
touch with heav- en, for my heart is al- read- y home!

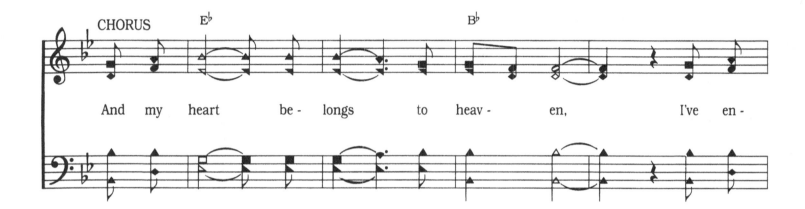

And my heart be- longs to heav- en, I've en-

trust- ed it all with the Lord; Tho my feet car- ry me an- y-

where I need to go, My heart is al- read- y home!

WHEN JESUS PASSED BY

Words and Music by
JEFF GIBSON

1. A crip-ple starts walk-ing, a blind man can see,
2. - I was a beg-gar in the rags of my sin,

A lep-er is cleansed and a cap-tive set free;
- Wealth-y with-out, oh, so need-y with-in;

A wo-man is re-joicing, her son did not die,
A king be-came my Sav-ior, now His rich-es are mine,

All these things hap-pened when Je-sus passed by.
I be-came God's child when Je-sus passed by.

CHORUS

When Je-sus passed by, when Je - sus passed by.

Gone were all the heart - aches, the trou - ble and strife.

Just reach out and touch Him,___ and He'll hear your cry;

Then you'll know some-thing hap-pened when Je - sus passed__ by.

BRING ME OUT OF THE DESERT

By LOIS TATUM

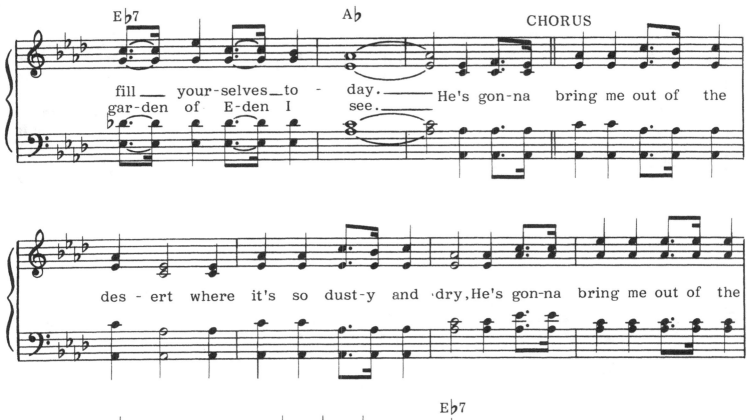

fill your-selves to - day. He's gon-na bring me out of the
gar-den of E-den I see.

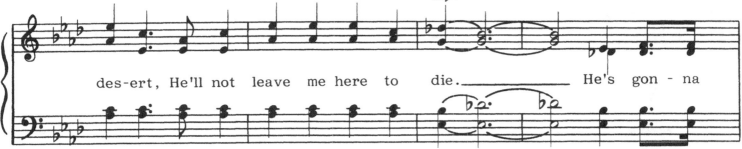

des - ert where it's so dust-y and dry, He's gon-na bring me out of the

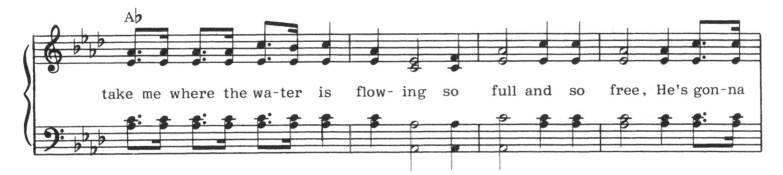

des-ert, He'll not leave me here to die. He's gon - na

take me where the wa-ter is flow-ing so full and so free, He's gon-na

bring me out of the des-ert and set my feet where they ought to be.

WALKING ON THE WATER

Words and Music by DAVID R. LEHMAN
and RUBY MOODY

1. Are we cruis-ing a-long, _ and _ tak-in' our ease _ while o-thers are a-
warm-ing the seat _ in the church where we go, _ do we take _ time to

stray? Some - times too bu-sy to reach out a hand _ to a
pray for the one who o-pens God's Ho-ly _ Book _ to be

neigh-bor a-cross _ the way? _ Have we told him a-bout _ _ sal-
giv-en _ the words to say? _ We can blame _ our-selves _ when the

va-tion's plan, _ or do we leave _ it up to the preach-er man? _ } Get
church is cold, _ start _ mov-ing for Je-sus and car-ry our load. }

out of the boat,__ start walk-ing on the wa-ter._____ Get

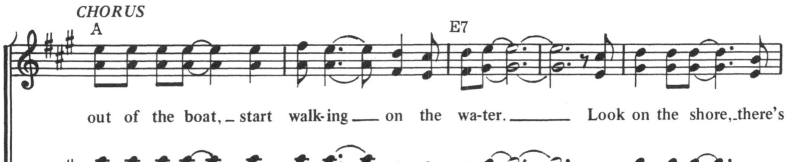

CHORUS

out of the boat,__ start walk-ing ____ on the wa-ter._____ Look on the shore,_there's

work for us__ to do._____ Get out of the boat,__ start

walk - ing on the wa-ter, _____ day's al-most gone,__ night's

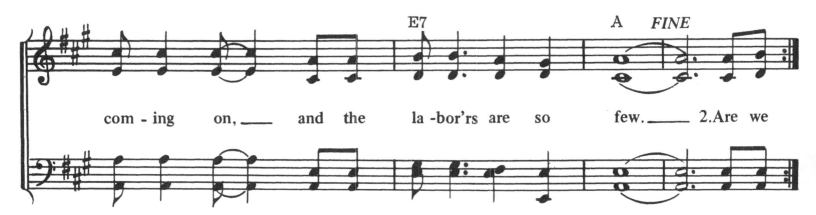

com - ing on, ___ and the la-bor'rs are so few.___ 2.Are we

TARRY HERE

By JEFF MORAN

1. It must have been a sad day for all His dis-
2. Now this road that I tra - vel some - times gets so

ci - ples when Je - sus was go - ing a - way.___
rock - y, it seems like I just can't go on.___

___ But as He rose through the clouds, ___ He left them this
___ But the thought cheers my heart when I stop to re-

mes - sage, ___ He said "I'll come back for you this same
mem - ber, ___ ver - y soon now we're all go - ing

way. _____
home. _____ Tar - ry here a lit - tle while, my

broth - er, _____ tar - ry here and _____ work while its

day. _____ Tar - ry here, it won't be much

long - er, _____ 'til I come back to

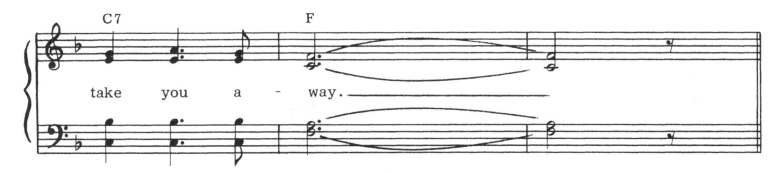

take you a - way. _____

JESUS, YOU JUST MADE MY DAY

By RUSSELL, ED
and JAMES EASTER

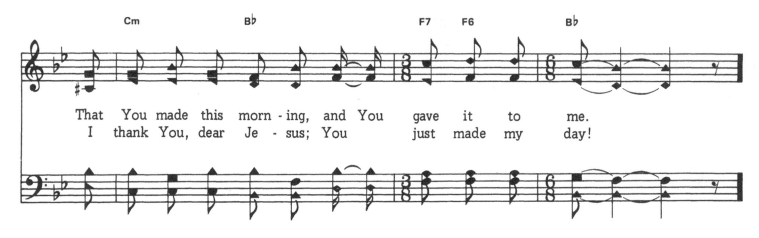

CHORUS

Je - sus, You just made my day, All my

dark clouds and bur - dens have all rolled a - way;

With joy all a - round me I'd just like to say, I'm

so thank - ful, Je - sus, You just made my day!

I AM WITH THEE

Words and Music by
JEFF GIBSON

1. I walked thru a valley so dark and so low,
2. I climbed up the mountain till I reached the top,

The sun did not shine there, but a lily did grow;
And there sprang a fountain in a dry, barren spot;

I cried to my Father, "How can this be?"
Again my heart questioned; my eyes could not see,

CHORUS

He said, "Can't you see, child? I am with thee!" I am with
Again Jesus whispered, "I am with thee!"

THE BROKEN ROSE

Words and Music by
SQUIRE E. PARSONS, JR.

I'M THE REASON

Words and Music by
COLBERT and JOYCE CROFT

1.I'm the beg - gar that stood by the way - side, ___
lone - ly in need of the Sav - ior, ___

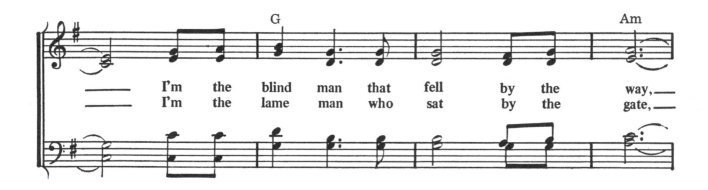

___ I'm the blind man that fell by the way, ___
___ I'm the lame man who sat by the gate, ___

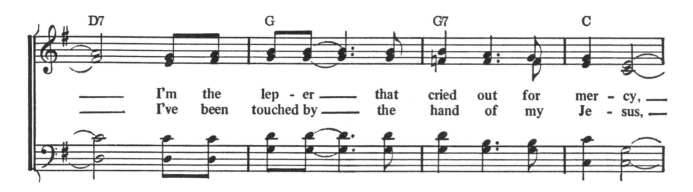

___ I'm the lep - er ___ that cried out for mer - cy, ___
___ I've been touched by ___ the hand of my Je - sus, ___

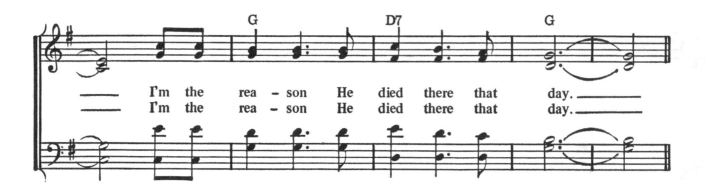

___ I'm the rea - son He died there that day. ___
___ I'm the rea - son He died there that day. ___

CHORUS

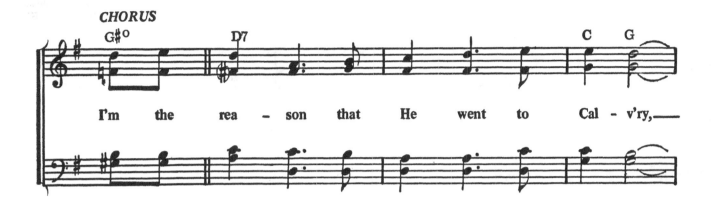

I'm the rea - son that He went to Cal - v'ry,____

____ I'm the rea - son for the old rug - ged cross.____

____ I'm the one who went a - stray, I'm the one who found His

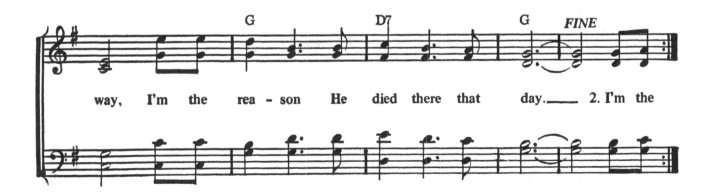

way, I'm the rea - son He died there that day.____ 2. I'm the

SOMEBODY TOUCHED ME

Words and Music by
SAVANA FOUST

IS THAT FOOTSTEPS THAT I HEAR

By COLBERT
and JOYCE CROFT

1. There is some - thing ____ that's gon - na hap - pen, and the day ____ is draw - ing near. It is time ____ to get ex - cit - ed, is that foot - steps that I hear? Come on, Gab - riel, blow your trum - pet, all the dead ____ in Christ shall

2. Are you read - y ____ for the rap - ture, when we meet ____ Him in the air? Oh, His com - ing ____ is draw - ing clos - er, is that foot - steps that I hear? Many a saint has fought the bat - tle, run the race, ____ and shed the

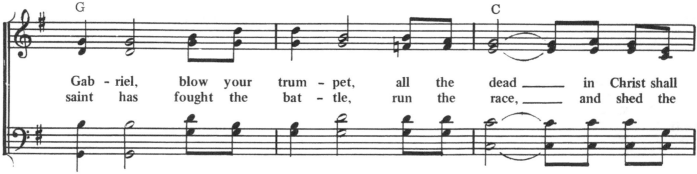

THEY'RE HOLDING UP THE LADDER

By The EASTER BROTHERS

I'M A JESUS FAN

Words and Music by
MIKE PAYNE

G

1. I was driv-ing home one Fri-day when com-mo-tion caught my ear,
(2. So I) drove a lit-tle fur-ther, and I saw an-oth-er crowd,
(3. So I) went to church that Sun-day, and I heard the preach-er say,

D7   **C**   **G**

In a field a crowd was gath-ered; I could hear them yell and cheer;
They were danc-ing, they were sway-ing; I heard mu-sic play-ing loud;
"Je-sus gave His life to save us, and He's com-ing back some day";

— "Tell me, why are you ex-cit-ed?" I asked a cer-tain man;
I asked a-gain, "Why get ex-cit-ed? I just don't un-der-stand!"
— So I start-ed get-ting hap-py; how I shout-ed how I cried,

D7   **C7**

He said, "There ain't no bet-ter rea-son—I'm a — foot-ball
— Some-one said, "Man, you're not with it! We're just — rock mu-sic
— Some-one said, "Don't get ex-cit-ed," oh, but this was my re-

WALK RIGHT OUT OF THIS VALLEY

By HAZEL TRUBEE

STANZAS

1. Now when the Lord let down the hedge on Job to try him, took
2. Well, now the road that we've got to trav-el to that cit-y, well,

all of his chil-dren and ev-'ry-thing that he owned, But, no,
it won't al-ways be on the moun-tain high, But you know the

Job did-n't sit down and cry, no, he lift-ed his head up high, And came
val-ley that we've got to face, — God said He's gon-na give us grace To come

out of that val-ley, thank God with a whole lot more.
up on the hill where the sun is shin-ing bright.

D. C. for chorus

SWEET BEULAH LAND

Words and Music by
SQUIRE PARSONS, JR.

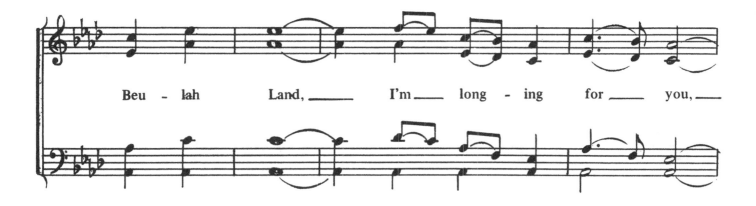

Beu - lah Land,_____ I'm_____ long - ing for_____ you,_____

_____ and some - day,_____ on _____ thee _____ I'll stand;_____

_____ There my home_____ shall _____ be_____ e - ter -

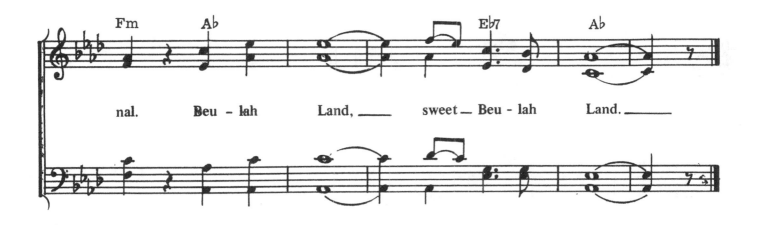

nal. Beu - lah Land,_____ sweet _____ Beu - lah Land._____

THE CITY COMIN' DOWN

Words and Music by
LAVANUL SHERRILL

1. Well, __ man has made __ a lot of things, __ — — They
2. Well, __ get your things __ to - geth - er, __ And walk out __
3. Well, there's New York Cit - y, Chi - ca - go, __ At - lan - ta and

look so fine, __ — — They're build-ing so __ high up in the sky __ they will
through the land, __ You're gon - na go __ on the rock - y moun - tain, __ gon - na
Bal - ti - more, __ — There's __ Den - ver and __ Tal - la - has - see, __ you can

al - most __ baf - fle your mind; __ But __ the time's gon-na turn, and they're all gon-na burn, __ and
cross on the des - sert sand; __ Well, __ Lot went __ down to __ Sod - dom, __ but
name them __ by __ the score; __ I don't __ have a __ big in - vest - ment, __ no

no - where __ will be found, __ I'm gon - na be up in that
not old __ A - bra - ham, __ He was __ look - in' for that cit - y __ that
man - sion __ way up town, __ But I've __ got one in that

CHORUS

John saw__ com-in' down.__ I'm not look-in' for a cit-y that's a-go-in' up,__ but the

one that's com-in' down,__ I'm not put-tin' my trust in the one that will crum-ble and

fall down to the ground;__ But I'm head-in' for the one that the Lord has made__ and is

built e-ter-nal-ly sound,__ I'm not look-in' for a cit-y go-

-in' up,__ but the one that's com-in' down.__

IT'S OUT OF THIS WORLD

By RONALD M. PAYNE

1. While trav-el-ing thru this world be - low, I see great cit-ies ev -'ry-where I
2. John saw_ that cit - y com-ing down, dressed like a bride_ in her wed - ding

go,_____ But I know that soon their beau-ty will fade_ a - way;_____
gown, He said that the walls are made of jas - per, the gates_ of pearl;_____

But there's a place wait-ing just for me, a cit - y that -'ll stand for e-ter-ni-
Where once a - gain God_ walks with man and dries_their_ tears with_ His_ own

ty, I'm tell-ing you the place_ where I'm go-ing is out of this world!_____
hand,

IN MY ROBE OF WHITE

Words and Music by
GENIECE SPENCER INGOLD

PRAISE GOD AND COUNTRY

Words and Music by DAVID R. LEHMAN
and CHARLES AARON WILBURN

THE SPIRIT WILL COME DOWN

Words and Music by
TIM HILL

I BOWED MY KNEES
(AND CRIED HOLY)

Arrangement by
JIMMIE DAVIS

1. I dreamed of a cit-y called glo-ry so bright and so fair, When I en-tered that gate I cried ho-ly; the an-gels all met me there; They car-ried me from man-sion to man-sion, and oh, what sights I saw! But I

2. I thought as I en-tered that cit-y my loved ones all knew me well, They showed me thru the streets of heav-en; such scenes too nu-m'rous to tell; I saw A-bra-ham, I-saac, and Ja-cob, Mark, Luke, and Tim-o-thy, But I

said, "I want to see Je - sus; He's the One who died for
said, "I want to see Je - sus; He's the One who died for

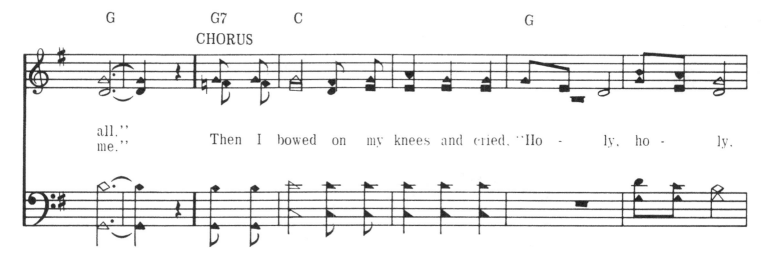

CHORUS

all." Then I bowed on my knees and cried, "Ho - ly, ho - ly,
me."

ho - ly, ho - ly, ho - ly, ho - ly;" Then I clapped my hands and sang,

"Glo - ry, glo - ry, Glo - ry to the Son of God!"

The <u>Only</u> Book of Inspirational Music You'll Ever Need!

Over 500 stimulating songs with special features like guitar chord frames and full lyrics make this a natural for any lover of gospel music!

MELODIES • LYRICS • CHORDS

This is the best and most complete book of gospel music ever compiled. "Gospel's Best" has something for everyone whether professional or amateur musician, choral group or accompanist — containing full lyrics for singers, guitar chord frames for guitar players and lead lines for piano, organ, guitar and all "C" instruments.

To help locate titles, two convenient indexes are provided:

- **Alphabetical** by song title.
- **Composer/Lyricist Index** — lists all composers and lyricists alphabetically followed by a list of their songs.

Look at this list of some of the titles included:

All My Trials • Because He Lives • El Shaddai • Cornerstones • Father's Eyes • He Touched Me • Home Where I Belong • How Great Thou Art • How Majestic Is Your Name • I Saw The Light • Miracle Man • My Tribute • Sing Your Praise To The Lord • A Thing Called Love • Through It All • Turn Your Radio On • What A Difference You've Made In My Life • Who Am I • You Needed Me.

The songs are representative of artists like:

Bill & Gloria Gathier • Andrae Crouch • Dottie Rambo • Larry Gatlin • Lanny Wolf • Johnny Cash • Albert E. Brumley • Rusty Goodman • many others.

HAL•LEONARD® CORPORATION

7777 W. BLUEMOUND RD. P.O. BOX 13819 MILWAUKEE, WI 53213